The New Sovereignty

The New Sovereignty

❖

Reginald Wallis

DIMENSION BOOKS
BETHANY FELLOWSHIP, INC.
Minneapolis, Minn. 55438

ISBN 0-87123-391-6

DIMENSION BOOKS
are published by Bethany Fellowship, Inc.
6820 Auto Club Rd.,
Minneapolis, Minnesota 55438

Printed in U.S.A.

PREFACE

The design of this book is to emphasize the all-important significance of the Lordship of Christ as the *condition and goal* of true regeneration. The inevitable effect of the new birth is that "He must reign." Salvation involves, in its very nature, heart consent to His sovereignty. This is an inviolate principle running right through the Word of God. The genuine Christian is one in whose heart the Lord has made a throne and a royal palace for himself.

The urge of this significant fact has been borne in upon the writer's heart with almost staggering significance of late. For many years he, like many others, regarded salvation as the automatic result of assenting to a scriptural proposition and believing certain facts.

If there is one plain truth with no uncertain sound, it is the weighty reality that *remission is never apart from submission*. There can be no *alliance without allegiance*. The Saviour is the Lord.

May the Holy Spirit enable writer and readers alike to appreciate the implications and appropriate the blessings of His sovereignty—and "so much the more as we see the day approaching."

Reginald Wallis

CONTENTS

HIS SOVEREIGNTY
IN RELATION TO:

INTRODUCTION

"Can a man receive Jesus Christ as his Saviour but not as his Lord?

Early in my ministry after a year of soul- and scripture-searching, I became convinced that Christ's sovereign government and His saving grace go together. "Him [Jesus] hath God exalted with his right hand to be a Prince and a Saviour" (Acts 5:31). Note the order. His position as a Prince precedes His power to pardon.

Previously I would have opposed such a statement. Intellectual honesty demanded a study of the issue. Thus began my spiritual safari through the New Testament in search of this truth. Careful study uncovered the fact that while Jesus Christ is mentioned 16 times as Saviour,

He is called Lord more than 470 times!

Well-known and used verses like Acts 16:31 took on a whole new edge: "Believe on the *Lord* Jesus Christ, and thou shalt be saved." The Lordship of Christ is not an option after salvation but a *condition for* and the *goal of* salvation.

Shortly after this Biblical exploration, the author's book "happened" to come to my hand. It was like a drink of cold water to a traveler! The author enlisted scripture after scripture and, marshalling them in phalanx strength, marched them by with invincible force.

Certain conclusions were inescapable. Though the teaching of an optional Lordship is not dead—it is deadly. In many cases it produces still-born "converts" who struggle with a false assurance of salvation. These have never settled the issue that *Christ is to be received as Lord* (Col. 2:6), and that's why they're in this fix. Let them say "yes" here and reality will begin.

I rejoice that this book is available again and recommend it to you. One word of caution: Reading this book could make you think from a new viewpoint. That kind of thinking can be dangerous, especially if you check it with scriptures. I know.

Elmer H. Murdoch
Omaha, Nebraska
December, 1973

CHAPTER I

HIS SOVEREIGNTY IN RELATION TO EVANGELISM

"That in all things he might have the pre-eminence."—Col. 1:18

A young Christian fellow was lying ill. He was on the borderland of glory. It was noticed by those standing by the sick-bed that, although very weak, he was trying feebly to articulate a sentence. They listened to catch the faintest whisper, but all they could hear was the one word "Bring . . ." They brought him water, but he signified that he did not want it. Again he said, "Bring . . ." so they brought his Bible. But he was past ability to read further. They then brought in his mother, but he was too near the end for seeing her. Suddenly his face lit up. Raising himself a little, he said in a clear ringing voice: "Bring forth the royal diadem, and crown Him Lord of all." Then, in another moment, he was with the Lord.

This simple and touching story indicates the supreme principle and purpose of redemption. The Word of God makes it perfectly clear that salvation's objective is intimately and indispensably related to the *sovereignty* of the Saviour in the believer's heart, in the Church, and ultimately in the universe. While salvation is without money and without price, it is not without conditions. Though it is utterly unmerited and all of grace, yet there is a predominant stipulation which the Holy Spirit associates with its possession and enjoyment. This is nothing less than the establishment of a new principle of divine Lordship, resulting in His sole right to the place of unrivalled preeminence in the heart. This is the "new creation" life in its innate substance and import. "Old things are passed away; behold, all things are become new" (II Cor. 5:17).

"All things new." Such newness of

life, with all its implications, is essentially the life of the risen Lord as head of His body, the church. It is an altogether distinct realm of life from that which is of the natural order. It finds its center in Christ, and its adequate development only as the unrivalled sovereignty of the risen Lord is acknowledged in the voluntary submission of heart and will to all His glorious purposes.

If it must be conceded that the life of the professing church of God on earth today is at a low spiritual ebb, may not the explanation be found, at least partially, in a failure to apprehend this sure and immutable principle of divine sovereignty? It is so very easy to presume upon the grace of God and even prostitute it by a kind of believism which affords dangerous ground for spiritual assumption. A counterfeit religious life is not only spiritually ineffective (in that it can never lead the soul into the blessings of His sovereignty), but it is positively hazardous.

But such an academic formality is not limited to a destructive criticism which denies the letter. It may also be expressed in a dead orthodoxy which denies the Spirit. While it is most important that we who humbly accept the Bible as the Word of God must ever "hold fast the form of sound words" (II Tim. 1:13), it must not be forgotten that this injunction is also followed by the important qualification: "In *faith and love* which is in Christ Jesus." How often zealous critics of the inspired Scriptures have looked for reality in the lives of the orthodox, and have not found it! They watched in vain for the evidences of true orthodoxy—love for and obedience to the One whom they profess to worship as their God, and whose word they unhesitatingly accept as their guide. Failing to discover this adorning of the doctrine, and in their blindness to the need of the new birth, they set up Jesus as Teacher and Example. May God deliver orthodox Christians from cold doctrines and a graceless contention for truth!

The enemy is a clever strategist, however, and it would seem that the real issue today centers rather less specifically around the rationalistic criticism of the Bible—for the archaeologist's spade has, of late, dug many holes in which to dispose of the skeletons of modernistic conjectures—but it focuses more definitely upon an evangelical appeal which may be purely psychic and emotional. He is not unduly perturbed by the impact of an evangelism in which the sovereignty of Christ is either eliminated or relegated to the background. But his challenging forces are ready for action wherever the preacher's evangel is calculated to lead souls to Calvary in submission and true faith.

Thank God for faithful messengers of God today whose one desire is the glory of God in the reclaiming of souls. It must not be forgotten, however, that mass evangelism is necessarily threatened with a peril of which every faithful preacher must be conscious. It is the tendency to an emotionalism which releases great waves of "soul" force, producing a "religious" agitation which may strongly resemble a movement of God. While Spirit-controlled emotionalism has its own appointed place in true evangelism, never was there greater need for a God-given discretion by which spiritual power may be discernible from a feverish religious excitement. It is conceded, of course, that a true, deep, convicting work of grace may be accompanied by emotional awakening. But such feelings are not in themselves a safe criterion of deep spiritual work in the heart. The enemy is ever ready to imitate the work of the Holy Spirit with religious stimulation which resembles real spirituality, but which leaves the soul empty and dissatisfied when the tide of excitement ebbs. Perhaps the greater tragedy is that it leaves an aftermath which necessarily generates its own problems! It stands to reason that souls who have become disillusioned are very much harder to influence subsequently with the real gospel message.

The possibility of such counterfeit emphasizes the supreme necessity of proclaiming a "new creation" life with no uncertain sound. It is a universal law that everything possessing productive power brings forth "after its kind." This is no less true in the ministry of holy things. Religious ministry may be psychic, orthodox, heretical, social, humanitarian, educational, political, or spiritual. In each case it produces results "after its kind." But are outward results, as such, the main objective of evangelism? God forbid! By those initiated into the art, results of a kind can be easily and cheaply produced. But the true end of evangelism is the establishment of Christ's sovereignty in the hearts of men. This is the work of the Holy Spirit, and it cannot be measured by statistics.

There is an ever-present danger of misunderstanding the heavenly character and essential *newness* of spiritual life. How important that its revolutionary and transforming inplications should be fully and clearly proclaimed! But how shall others hear without the preaching? If those who are entrusted with the truth fail adequately to interpret the doctrines of God, is it surprising that there should be distressing ignorance concerning the necessary inplications of true discipleship? How vitally important it is, therefore, that ministers of the Word of God should themselves "prove all things," seek the illumination of the Holy Spirit, labor in the "ability which God giveth," and earnestly see to it that natural gifts and powers of personality are animated and dominated by the life of Him whom God has raised from the dead!

On the other hand, it must not be overlooked that an utter sanctification "for their sakes" does not necessarily ensure the elimination of all unreality, for disappointments and spurious conversions are also experienced in pure spiritual evangelism of the highest order. The Lord himself made it quite clear that the gospel net would contain bad as well as good fish, i.e., there would be spurious professions as well as real conversions. But it is surely part of the sacred trust committed to the gospel messenger that, so far as in him lies, he should *reduce to a minimum* the possibility of such an element of unreality. His main business is to exalt Christ by a faithful testimony, conscious that true conversion must ever be the work of the Holy Spirit himself.

Now it will not be deduced from these facts that the evangelist's business is to go to the other extreme and consistently refuse to draw in the net! Surely that is an essential part of the fisherman's task. It does mean that his primary objective will be to glorify the Lord at all costs, and by the proclamation of an uncompromising evangel labor for a deep and definite work of grace in the hearts of his hearers.

CHAPTER II

HIS SOVEREIGNTY
IN RELATION TO
THE ETERNAL PURPOSE

"That . . . he might gather together in one all things in Christ."—Eph. 1:10

What is the great objective upon which the heart of God is set? It is vitally important that this should be scripturally apprehended. What is the chief end of the divine activity for this age and even unto the "ages of the ages"? A plain utterance of the Holy Spirit in Ephesians 1:9-11 makes it quite clear.

> Having made known unto us the mystery of his will according to his good pleasure which he hath purposed in himself:
> That in the dispensation of the fulness of times he might gather together in one

all things in Christ, both which are in heaven, and which are on earth; *even* in him:

In whom also we have obtained an inheritance, being predestinated according to the purpose of him who worketh all things after the counsel of his own will.

Manifestly the unrivalled supremacy of the Son of God is the objective upon which the heart of God is set. All things must be consummated and gathered together in one in Christ. He must have the pre-eminence in all things "both which are in heaven and which are on earth." If it is God's will, therefore, that all men should be saved (I Tim. 2:4), does it not follow that the sovereignty of Christ is intimately related to the condition and the goal of salvation? A heart recognition of His right to reign, together with a full consent to all that is thereby involved, is the supreme principle of the "new creation" life. It is at once the effect and the evidence of the new birth.

Though the eternal purpose is ordained to complete an absolute realization, there is manifested another challenging will which is set defiantly against the will of God. The redemption story centers round an age-long conflict between these two opposing wills. While the eternal decree will find its sure consummation in the universal sovereignty of the Son of God, another voice is heard which treacherously aims at its abrogation. Lucifer, son of the morning (Isa. 14), daringly shakes his fist in the face of the Most High and declares, "I *will* be as God!" The first Adam was created as head of the human race, one in whom the divine purpose and pleasure would center. He was to have dominion as God's vice-regent upon the earth. But the subtle maneuvering of the enemy caused him, through transgression, to forfeit the sovereignty. That old serpent, the devil, cunningly usurped the allegiance of one who had been created for God's glory, and thereby seized the crown rights.

Does this mean, however, that the divine end is forever thwarted? No, God's eternal purpose must be ultimately realized:

> For the Lord of Hosts hath purposed, and who shall disannul it? and his hand is stretched out, and who shall turn it back? (Isa. 14:27)

The sovereignty must be restored, but how? There is only one way: the mighty usurper must himself be overthrown, a task which only the Almighty God could undertake. Around this central fact lies the great redemptive message of the Gospel. The decree found its *inauguration* in the heart of God before the foundation of the world; its *first expression* in the mystery of the incarnation; its *demonstration* in a life of unsullied purity; and its *basic consummation* in the death, resurrection, ascension and glorification of the Son of God. God became manifest in the flesh. For 33 1/2 years the God-Man demonstrated His essential deity and Lordship by supremacy over the world, the flesh, and the devil.

It will be profitable to trace briefly this glorious fact through the gospel story, and see how constantly the Holy Spirit declares the majesty and sovereignty of the Son of God. Here is a voice crying in the wilderness, a herald of One who was to come and whose shoelaces the forerunner was not worthy to unloose. John the Baptist is preparing "the way of *the Lord*" (Matt. 3:3).

Who is He in yonder stall
At whose feet the shepherds fall?
'Tis the Lord, the King of Glory,
'Tis the Lord, O wondrous story!

On the first happy Christmas Day, as the shepherds are watching their flocks by night, the angel of the Lord announces the glorious news: "Unto you is born . . . a Saviour, which is Christ *the Lord*" (Luke 2:11).

Who is this marvelously taught Boy who discusses important ecclesiastical matters with the learned doctors of the synagogue? He is the *Son*, who must be about His Father's business (Luke 2:49).

Then, at the outset of His public ministry, His deity and sonship are irrefutably proclaimed from heaven as He is baptized of John in the Jordan, and the Holy Spirit descends upon Him in bodily shape like a dove. "This is my beloved *Son* in whom I am well pleased" (Matt. 3:17).

Throughout His entire earthly ministry, Jesus ever claimed oneness with the Father (John 14:9). Who is this mighty Miracle Worker? Take one example and listen to the leper's confession: "Lord, if thou wilt, thou canst make me clean" (Matt 8:2). And thus we might trace it right through. The uniform testimony of the Holy Spirit in the earthly narrative establishes His unimpeachable sovereignty.

But it is important to note that this divine determination to establish the preeminence of the Son of God is demonstrated in the incessant antagonism of the devil, who directs his strategy against the present implications and the final establishment of *Christ's sovereignty.* Throughout our Lord's earthly sojourn, this was the battlefield upon which the conflict ceaselessly raged. In the wilderness temptations, the constant appeal was "*If* thou be the Son of God." The enemy's great objective was to violate His supremacy by securing an admission of inferiority from the lips of the Son of God. Thus, he defiantly claimed the worship due only to the Godhead.

> Therefore the Jews sought the more to kill him, because he not only had broken the Sabbath, but *said also that God was his Father, making himself equal with God.* (John 5:18. See also John 7:29.)

Further, Satan resumes his attack with increasing intensity as the shadow of the Cross rests heavily upon the Saviour. In the final scene, the relentless usurper makes his last frantic onslaught (Matt. 27:4-43). When the devil-inspired and misled people clamor for His death, the issue again focuses on His claim to deity.

> And they began to accuse him, saying, We found this *fellow* perverting the nation, and forbidding to give tribute to Caesar, saying that he himself is Christ a king. (Luke 23:2. See also Luke 22:67-71; 23:35)

Why did they ultimately crucify Him? Did they object to His mighty works, the fact that He "went about doing good"? No, indeed! There was an element of satisfaction in all this which appealed to the popularity of the crowd. That was not of primary consequence at this point. Let it be deeply engraved on every mind and heart that the one issue of vital consequence was the assertion of His *right to sovereignty*. With that issue in clear perspective, the final decision is clear and unequivocal. "*We will not*"—what? "We will not have this man

28

to *reign* over us." "We have no king but Caesar." Obviously, that was the leading factor resulting in His death. They *crucified* Him because they would not *crown* Him. This has been, and ever will be, the supremest of all issues for all men at all times: *Coronation or Crucifixion.*

Thus, the great conflict of the ages continues to this day. The devil's paramount objective is to rob the God-Man of His sovereign rights. His twentieth-century tactics differ from his old-time maneuvers, but the one supreme purpose remains unchanged. The object of modern destructive criticism, for example, is to drag down the Saviour from His pinnacle of deity. The modernist will concede that Jesus was a good man, a noble example, and a great leader. But when it comes to His claim to be Christ the *Lord*, the Sent-One from God, one with the Father, attesting His credentials by heavenly miracles, dying a sacrificial death of infinite value to God and to men, rising again in the power of an endless and sinless life, ever living to intercede, and returning again in glorious power, there is at once the inevitable and ever-manifest *protest of the natural heart!* It is the same old issue.

One of the diabolical signs of the end-time of this age will be false claimants to the worship which is due only to the Godhead. Said the Saviour: "Many shall come in my name, saying, I am the Christ." Nor do they merely claim to be Jesus, be it noted. This is nothing less than a counterfeit demand for a sovereignty which rightly belongs to the anointed King. In the final count, however, Satan *must* bow, and the true believer may antedate with joy the approach of "the end, when he shall have delivered up the kingdom to God, even the Father; when he shall have put down all rule and all authority and power. For he must reign, till he hath put all enemies under his feet" (I Cor. 15:24-25).

CHAPTER III

HIS SOVEREIGNTY IN RELATION TO NATURE

"What manner of man is this, that even the winds and the sea obey him!"—Matt. 8:27

Notice also how marvelously the sovereignty of the Saviour is demonstrated in the realm of nature. The disciples are in the midst of a terrible storm. They are terrified lest they should be swallowed up by the waves, and realize that they possess no resources but in His power. First rebuking them for their little faith, He then asserts His supremacy as the Lord of creation by rebuking the winds and the waves. At the sound of His omnipotent voice they subside, and there is a great calm. Was not this, just as every other miracle which He performed, a sign of His Lordship?

But still more striking are the illustrations of His preeminence in that realm of nature wherein the first Adam had received jurisdiction, but failed. Made in the divine image and after that likeness, he was to "have dominion over the fish of the sea, and over the fowl of the air, and over every living thing that moveth on the earth." Here is a threefold realm of nature—sea, air and earth, with their inhabitants of fish, fowl and flesh. But in each realm the first Adam failed. The Holy Spirit is careful, therefore, to record specific illustrations of the sovereignty of the "last Adam" in each of these domains. It is not surprising that each of the three instances we shall note is recorded in the Gospel of Matthew—the gospel of His sovereignty.

1. *Fish.* In Matthew 27:27, we read a striking incident in connection with the paying of tribute. The Saviour told one of His fisherman-followers to go to the sea, cast in his hook, and lo, in the mouth of the fish which would be hooked would

be found a piece of money! Thus it turned out to be! Who but the sovereign, omnipotent Lord of the seas could have contrived to perform such an aquatic marvel? It was His mighty power and sovereign preordination that constrained Peter to cast in the hook just at the precise spot, and to guarantee that a particular fish, containing in its mouth a coin which was evidently too big for its gullet, should be there at that precise moment, ready to bite! Yes, this was the work of the Governor of the "seas and all that therein is."

Again, in John 21 we have the record of a whole night's fishing which resulted in nothing but tired limbs and heavy hearts. What a commentary on man's loss of ascendancy in this realm! Not a single fish entered the net. They had toiled all night and caught nothing. But the same mighty Lord welcomes them in the morning and bids them cast the net again, but it must be "on the right side" this time! He then adds a sublime guarantee of success: "Ye shall find!" They obeyed, and it was even as He had ordained! "They cast therefore, and now they were not able to draw it for the multitude of fishes" (vs. 6). John is so overcome that he is limited to one comment, which is an explanation as well as an exclamation: "It is the Lord!" Yes, it was a wonderful exemplification of a regained sovereignty. The fishes were commanded and they obeyed. Only the omnipotent Lord could have designed that this draught of fishes, just so many, should have been ready for the net at that specific time, and at the very spot where the disciples would choose to lower it!

2. *Fowl.* After the Lord had partaken of the Passover feast with His disciples (Matt. 26) and referred again to His impending death and resurrection, Peter passionately declares that although all should be offended, yet will he not deny his Master. He would even die with Him! In reply, the Saviour prophesies Peter's failure, and associates his threefold denial with the crowing of a cock. This particular bird would act according to Christ's sovereign will, and would unwittingly be present at a particular place and a particular time, for a particular

34

purpose. For a predetermined period the cock would remain silent, but at the precise moment of Peter's third denial it would stretch its neck to sound a voice of rebuke! The bird was commanded and it obeyed. Thus it happened "immediately" (vs. 75), for this is the Man who regains the lost dominion over the fowl of the air as well as the fish of the sea.

3. *Flesh.* In preparation for His triumphal entry into Jerusalem, the Lord sent two disciples into a nearby village, and told them that on entering they would find an ass tied (Matt. 21). Mark's account adds the significant remark: "a colt tied, *whereon never man sat.*" Therein lies the phenomenon of His sovereignty. This was an untried animal, wild and untamed, not yet broken in! Was it not a miracle that such an animal should patiently suffer Christ to ride upon him? The Saviour instructs His messengers to bring the animal to Him. If asked why they were doing so, they were to preclude every possible objection by saying, "The Lord hath need of him." Exactly as He had said, so they found it. Loosing the animal, they bring it to

Him. Then, placing a covering on the ass, they set the Saviour upon it, and with fitting decorum He proceeds to ride into the city! Was such a thing ever heard of before? Here is an untamed colt—wild, headstrong and unruly in spirit—quite unnaturally submissive and under perfect control. Who else but the Lord himself, with any concern for self-respect, would have undertaken such a journey by such means? Only He *could* do it. Was He not the sinless Sovereign?

Is not the ferocity of animal nature one of the results of sin? We read that in the coming Golden Age of His undisputed sway, when He exercises His right to world sovereignty, the rapacious nature of the brute creation shall be universally subdued. Then "the wolf also shall dwell with the lamb, and the leopard shall lie down with the kid; and the calf and the young lion and the fatling together; and a little child shall lead them; and the cow and the bear shall feed; their young ones shall lie down together ... *They shall not hurt* ... for the earth shall be full of the knowledge of the Lord as the waters cover the sea" (Isa. 11:6-9). The

36

whole creation shall acknowledge His Lordship.

Yes, the meek and lowly One who rides upon an ass is none other than the sovereign Lord to whom all things have been put into subjection. He rides the untamed beast with such kingly dignity that the people spread their garments on the ground and acclaim His Majesty with homage: "Hosanna in the highest!"

Thus the Lord from heaven presents His credentials of sovereignty in the realm of nature: "He is *Lord* of all."

CHAPTER IV

HIS SOVEREIGNTY IN RELATION TO REDEMPTION

". . . where also our Lord was crucified."—Rev. 11:8

The Lordship of Christ is also emphasized by the Holy Spirit in relation to the eternal redemptive sacrifice of Calvary. Standing by the Cross, we see Him accomplishing the great objective for which He came into the world. Tackling the sin question once and for all, He accomplishes a mighty triumph over the prince of death, and in many scriptures there is presented to us an unequivocal testimony to His sovereignty. Who is this glorious person hanging upon a Roman gibbet, covered with shame and ignominy, and suffering the most unspeakable torture of body and spirit? "It is Christ [the anointed One] who died" (Rom. 8:34). This is something more than the earthly cutting off of a very wonderful individual whose name was Jesus. It is "the dying of the LORD Jesus" (II Cor. 4:10). It is the God-Man who thus sinks to the awful depths of Calvary.

This was no ordinary cross. Many criminals have suffered such an ignominious death. But *this* Cross is unique, and its matchless glory lies in the fact that the One who hung upon it is himself the sovereign Lord. It is "the Cross of our LORD Jesus Christ." Because of the matchless glory and sovereignty of the Cross-bearer himself, the hill outside the city wall has been the rendezvous of multitudes from every clime and nation and color down through the ages. Only here can a holy God meet with unholy sinners. Sin-stained feet, weary with life's journey and its burdens, have found their way to this sacred spot, and passed on again with the hearts light and faces aglow. Why? Because it is the place of pardon, peace and cleansing. It is "the place where our Lord was crucified" (Rev. 11:8). It was at that moment of His supreme humiliation, when it seemed that His death was a triumphant check-mating by the devil, that even His enemies acclaim His sovereignty. "Truly this man was the *Son of God.*" The life of the sovereign Lord was not taken from Him (John 10:18), but He chose to lay it down of himself.

Wonderful indeed is the divine strategy which forces from His antagonists the truth contained in the words of the super-scription: "THIS IS THE KING OF THE JEWS" (Luke 23:38). When the chief priests remonstrated with Pilate for such an unqualified avowal, his reply was final: "What I have written I have written." Pilate had previously asked: "What *is* truth?" Here, he was verily pronouncing it!

But they who visit this spot to gaze at the crucified One, having bowed their heads in reverent wonder, look up again to discover that the Cross in now empty! His sinless humanity and acknowledged deity has proclaimed His sovereignty over death, and on the bright resurrection morn both the Cross and the tomb are destitute.

Who tears the bars of death asunder and conquers the grave forever? How many verses leap into our minds in the apostolic records! We shall have occasion to refer later to Peter's testimony on the Day of Pentecost. "Let all the house of Israel know assuredly, that God hath made that same Jesus, whom ye have crucified, both *Lord and Christ*" (Acts 2:36). It is the Lord who arose from the dead. "With great power gave the apostles witness of the resurrection of the Lord Jesus" (Acts 4:33). In glorious triumph He ascends to the Father's throne, becomes the center of heaven's admiration and worship, and is divinely ordained to be "head over all things to the church, which is his body . . ." (Eph. 1:22-23).

Yes, it is the Lord! The greater David defeated the greater Goliath, and by His death "destroyed him that had the power of death" (Heb. 2:14). All through the mighty program, from the manger of

41

humility to the majesty of conquest, He never fails to establish the divine glory of His person.

Thus, the atoning work accomplished, the Holy Spirit proceeds to establish the supremacy of the risen Lord in the constituting of a Kingdom in dual form. The regained sovereignty must find adequate expression throughout the ages of time and on into eternity. During this age of grace, the Kingdom may be said to be in *mystery*, for God is taking out from the world "a people for his name" (Acts 15:14). The Lordship of Christ is now being demonstrated by the Holy Spirit in a spiritual organism called "the Church," and in the heart of every believer so incorporated into that Church by regeneration (Eph. 4:4-6). "To us," says the apostle, "there is one Lord Jesus Christ" (I Cor. 8:6).

In the very nature of the case, therefore, the Son of God must *come again*, thus demonstrating His sovereignty further by the release of His people, the transforming of the mortal to immortality, and the corruptible to the incorruptible. As He exemplified His Lordship over death at the graveside of Lazarus, so shall He come again to utter a shout of universal victory, "Come forth!" The dead shall be raised and the living shall be changed. For whom, then, do we look? Again, observe the Holy Spirit's testimony to His sovereignty. While it is ever "this same Jesus"—the Man of Galilee and Calvary—who shall come again, this mighty event is nothing less than "the coming of the *Lord*" (James 5:7). He is the "blessed and only Potentate, the King of kings, and Lord of lords" (I Tim. 6:15). (Read also Phil. 3:20; 4:5; I Thess. 4:15-17; Jude 14; Rev. 22:20.) This is the very One who "hath on his vesture and on his thigh a name written, KING OF KINGS, and LORD OF LORDS" (Rev. 19:16). The echoing prayer of the Church is: "Even so, come, *Lord* Jesus" (Rev. 22:20).

CHAPTER V

HIS SOVEREIGNTY
IN RELATION TO
THE NEW BIRTH

"Except a man be born again, he cannot see the kingdom of God."—John 3:3

In view of what we have already observed, it is now necessary to consider the real nature and main implications of that mighty miracle of regeneration by which the sons of men may be redeemed and brought into eternal co-operation with God in His great purposes. If the heart of God is set upon the acknowledged sovereignty and undisputed preeminence of His dear Son, then it reasonably follows that fellowship with the Father and His Son Jesus Christ must necessarily involve *oneness of purpose* in such a design and intention. This is utterly impossible on the natural plane, for "the natural man is enmity against God." Every child of Adam is born in sin and "shapen in iniquity," alienated from the life of God, and antagonistic to Him by nature. Since He is controlled by that spirit of enmity which characterizes the devil himself and all his seed (Gen. 3:15), *new birth* becomes a divine imperative. Darkness can have no fellowship with light.

Regeneration is the one and only avenue into a new realm of divine life, and only by virtue of this new creation life is co-operation with God possible. "Being born again" (I Pet. 1:23) is something infinitely bigger than being pardoned and made happy. It is being "called unto the fellowship" (I Cor. 1:9). It is being *brought to God* (I Pet. 3:18). It is a call henceforth to *walk with God* (Rev. 3:4). It is a *transfer of heart allegiance*. It necessarily involves submission to the rule of another kingdom. It is an altogether new realm of sovereignty and a change of ownership. Speaking to Nicodemus, the Saviour said: "Except a man be born again, he cannot see *the kingdom* of God" (John 3:3). The new birth of a soul is nothing less than the subjugation of a rebel of earth and his transformation into a loyalist of heaven. There are no rebels in the *Kingdom* of God. The new birth is revolutionary. Hitherto, other lords have had dominion; sin and self have reigned upon the throne of the heart; the spirit of disobedience has been actively at work; the devil has dominated his helpless slaves and executed his dark designs through "the children of wrath." But regeneration effects the mighty transformation of a new heart and a new center of life. Henceforth, Christ is Lord and *He must reign.*

Every child of Adam is by nature a servant of sin, just as surely as the children of Israel were in helpless slavery to a cruel taskmaster in Egypt. Their salvation by Passover blood and the Red Sea passage meant not only escape from the judgment that fell upon Egypt, but it meant *release from the tyranny of Pharaoh.* The type is adequate and beautiful. The believer's redemption by the blood of Christ is not only salvation from divine judgment upon sin, but it implies the institution of a new sovereignty. It is release from former tyranny. True conversion is the *initial* expression of loyalty to the heavenly King on the part of one who has hitherto lived in rebellion.

On enlistment a soldier swears allegiance to his king, thereby placing himself at the disposal of high authority. Joining the army means utter repudiation of a former program which was self-governed and self-chosen, and full acquiescence in a new order of things. He is no longer his own. In this matter there is no alternative, no middle ground. The believer, by virtue of a faith that implies *willingness to obey*, is no longer the captain of his own soul or the master of his own destiny. His entrance into "the kingdom of God's dear Son" essentially implies submission to the orders of the King. Though introduced into a sphere of perfect liberty, he is henceforth under law to Christ, whose service is perfect freedom. He is bought with a price. He is part of a "purchased possession." "One is your *master*, even Christ" (Matt. 23: 8).

The alternative to salvation is condemnation. But why are men condemned? It is not primarily because they *do not want to be saved*, but because they continue in rebellion and WILL NOT acknowledge the divine sovereignty. Eternal perdition is the inevitable consequence of a persistent and unpardoned spirit of rebellion. "Ye *will not* come UNTO ME that ye might have life." Refusing to come to Him is nothing less than the repudiation of His Lordship. Such is the inevitable and unswerving bias of the human heart. Listen to the divine pronouncement on this point:

> But those mine enemies, *which would not that I should reign over them,* bring hither, and slay them before me. (Luke 19:27)

Can it be thought for a moment that the reception of eternal life (or of Him who is the life) involves anything less than heart consent to His sovereignty? The blessing of salvation must never be detached from the sovereignty of the

Blesser. His gifts are never divorced from His government. Indeed, it is because He is who He is that salvation is possible at all. There is "none other name." "His name shall be called . . . the Prince of Peace. Of the increase of His government and peace there shall be no end" (Isa. 9:6-7). Is it not an obvious paradox to expect the *riches* of the kingdom apart from the *rights* of the King? If a person desires the privileges of an earthly society or organization, must he not first of all join the society and thereby consent to the rules which govern the rights?

In one of the all-too-rare treatments of this subject in Christian literature today, Mr. George Goodman, in his excellent book *Great Truths Simply Stated,* illustrates the inconsistency of man's claim to rest on the finished work of Christ while refusing in practical life to own His kingship. He writes as follows:

> A king has part of his kingdom in rebellion, and in order to show his grace causes mercy to be proclaimed to the rebels on their yielding to him and seeking reconciliation on the ground

of the proclamation. He threatens destruction to those who continue to defy his authority. One of the rebels is warned of his danger, and replies, "I am in no danger; I am resting on the proclamation; I am sure the King is faithful; he will never break his promise nor withdraw his proclaimed mercy."

"But you are still in rebellion, you are continuing in the course he condemns, and are indifferent to his commands, and the mercy is offered to those who yield."

"True, but the mercy is free, there are no conditions, and to make conditions would be to make it no more of grace," is the reply.

What should we say to such reasoning? Alas, is it not in effect the language of some who, while refusing Christ as Lord, yet profess to trust in Him and His work for Salvation?

Thus, the principle of the new birth is the *acknowledged sovereignty of Christ in the heart*. It is earnestly affirmed that any religious experience, however thrilling or realistic, which leaves the soul short of heart consent to the Lordship of Christ, cannot be true regeneration. There is no greater danger in Christendom today than mistaking an *emotional religious crisis* for real entrance into newness of life. Walter Marshall on *Sanctification* (*circ.* 1660) wrote:

Why doth a man seek a pardon if he intend to go on in rebellion and stand out in defiance of his Prince? They seek a pardon in a mocking way and intend not to return unto obedience. . . .

To take a part of His Salvation and leave out the rest? But Christ is not divided. . . .

They would be saved by Christ and yet be out of Christ in a fleshly state, whereas God doth free none from condemnation but those who are in Christ.

This immutable principle finds striking expression in the Holy Spirit's narrative of the conversion of Saul of Tarsus on the Damascus road. Here is a religionist whose eyes were blinded by the "god of this age," suddenly stricken down in mighty conviction of sin, and subdued by a heavenly light above the brightness of the sun. In a moment of time Saul, the religious bigot, becomes Paul the saint, by nothing less than a revelation of the Lordship of Christ. The One who declared "I am Jesus" is immediately revealed as *the risen Lord*. This mighty unveiling of the glorified Christ reduces the man to zero and extracts from him the first expression of a new-found life: "Lord, what wilt thou have me to do?" True conversion is also a commission. This man had been captured and captivated. Henceforth he repudiates any claim to rule his own life or any right to govern his own program. The One who died and rose again had so enchanted this fanatic of religion that his one slogan for all time must be "henceforth ... *unto him!*" (II Cor. 5: 15). Yes, this is the essential principle of conversion. Nothing less than this is implied in the new birth. "To me to live *is Christ*. It is no longer I, but Christ liveth in me."

The conversion of Lydia, the purple-seller of Thyatira (Acts 16.) affords a striking contrast in divine operation, but leads to the same objective. With nothing spectacular or sensational as an accompaniment to her faith, she receives salvation as unostentatiously as a flower opens up to the warm rays of the sun. With quiet dignity her conversion is described by the Holy Spirit in the little sentence "whose heart the Lord opened."

She worshipped God, and desired to be found "faithful to the Lord."

When the Lord Jesus presented himself to the sorrowing Martha as the resurrection and the life, He called for an affirmation from her heart and lips as to who He was. Notice the answer: "I believe that thou art *the Christ,* the *Son of God*" (John 11:27). Thus was her confession. Thus, in these instances and others, there is divine reiteration of the inviolate principle that sovereignty governs salvation.

Who, then, is really born of God? Notice carefully the scriptural answer: "Whosoever believeth that Jesus is *the Christ* is born of God" (I John 5:1). It is "The Christ," be it noted. While the Saviour is ever the Christ, it is clear that His saviourhood is indissolubly related to His sovereignty. On the other side, "Who is a liar but he that denieth that Jesus is the Christ?" (I John 2:22). The One who saves is the anointed One, the Sent-One of God, the Messiah, the King! Here are some of His wonderful titles in the Scriptures:

Almighty God
Alpha and Omega
Beginning of the Creation of God
Blessed and Only Potentate
King of Kings
Lord of Lords
Captain of our Salvation
Everlasting Father
Governor of Israel
Heir of All Things
King of Nations
Lion of the Tribe of Judah
The Mighty God
The Only Begotten Son
Prince of Peace
The Son of God
God over All
The Eternal God
Jehovah
Lord of Hosts
King of Glory

He is the One before whom all heaven bows in reverent homage. One day His glory will flood the universe. This is my Saviour! *"My Lord and my God."*

In a chorus written by the late Dr. J. Stuart Holden, he puts a simple but adequate prayer into the lips of one who seeks pardon and cleansing, and who recognizes that the impartation of these blessings is only possible on the ground of His sovereignty:

> Cleanse me from my sin, *Lord*;
> Put Thy power within, *Lord*;
> Take me as I am, *Lord*,
> And make me *all Thine own*;
> Keep me day by day, *Lord*,
> Underneath *Thy sway, Lord*:
> *Make my heart Thy Palace*
> *And Thy royal throne.*

Salvation is the beginning of discipleship. What is a disciple but one who bows to discipline? To be a follower of the Saviour necessarily involves a willingness to say "Amen" to His commands. His terms of discipleship have never been abrogated or abridged. They embrace the denial of self, the taking up of the Cross, and a yielding to the sovereignty of Him whom the disciple acknowledged as Lord. It is something more than salvation from "the *penalty* of sin" (an expression not found in Scripture); it is redemption from "all iniquity" (Titus 2:14), and that is only possible by the indwelling life of the risen Lord.

But there is a matter arising here which needs to be explicitly understood.

It is not suggested for a moment that every new-born soul does (or could) possess a full intellectual apprehension of all that is implied by sovereignty of the Saviour. Such an unfolding is a life experience of ever-deepening spirituality and soul-development. Indeed, it could safely be affirmed that a mental understanding of the sovereignty of Christ is not a necessary accompaniment of true faith. Many are truly born again who know little or nothing of the theology of divine sovereignty. Salvation is not primarily a matter of the intellect, but of the heart. If the Holy Spirit produces saving faith in the heart, enabling its exercise and bringing it to fruition, then the great transaction is done, irrespective of the measure of intellectual conception of theological facts. To believe in the heart is to receive Jesus as Lord (Rom. 10:9), after which the Holy Spirit, working in the soul the obedience of faith, will lead it into fuller apprehension and revelation.

As a case in point, what could the dying thief have understood of the implications of Christ's sovereignty? Yet his conversion at the end of a godless life is nothing less than a spiritual expression of this very thing. Seeing his need of a Saviour and acknowledging his sin in heart repentance, the Holy Spirit at once enlightens him as to the deity of the One who hangs by his side, and he cries out with humble confidence: "Lord, remember me!"

It would be well, at this point, to enquire into the real meaning of faith. True faith must ever lead the soul to submission of heart and life to the sovereign Lord. But here the red flag of warning must be hoisted high in regard to the danger of mere believism. While believing, or faith, is the one and only instrument of salvation, it is vitally important that we should understand what God means by it.

Faith is not merely an assent of the mind to the great doctrinal verities of the Gospel, though such an assent is necessary to true faith. While God has given to men His final word in matters relating to salvation, it must be remembered that faith is something more than the intellectual reception of these facts.

Faith has to do with a Person, and He is the sovereign Lord. It is the reception of Him of whom the facts speak. Orthodoxy of creed, though absolutely essential, must not be mistaken for the enthronement of Christ in the heart. Any student of Scripture may acquire extensive knowledge of Bible history and doctrine, may even believe it all to be quite authoritative, yet be utterly devoid of divine life. Why? Because Life is in the Person and not in the proposition. Believing a text of Scripture to be true is not synonymous with receiving the Christ of the text. It is good to know the Book of the Lord, but salvation is knowing the Lord of the Book.

May it not be that this touches the basic secret of failure with many who know and accept the truth of the Gospel? They are urged, and rightly so, to "believe and be saved." They *do* believe, and believe sincerely, yet nothing vital happens! There is no change of heart. In most cases, such disappointment is the normal result of wrong or inadequate believing, scripturally referred to as "believing in vain." It is one of the devil's favorite substitutes for saving faith. To know the Scriptures "from a child" is, indeed, an untold blessing, but if the truth received into the mind is not quickened into life by the Holy Spirit, how deadening can that truth become! There is a difference between truth and *the* truth. Truth is comprised of facts. *The* truth is a Person (John 14:6). The former is the divinely ordained agency of introduction to the latter. Unless the *written* Word leads me to bow in submission to the *living* Word, it can only bring me into judgment. Beware of this kind of only believism. It is not the text that saves, but the One of whom the text speaks.

Can it therefore be doubted that the Saviour who shed His blood to redeem is essentially the risen Lord who reigns? *Submission to Him* is the one and only basis of *remission by Him.* There is no *alliance* without *allegiance.* Speaking of Israel, Paul declares that their failure is due to the fact that they "have not submitted themselves unto the righteousness of God" (Rom. 10:3).

CHAPTER VI

HIS SOVEREIGNTY
IN RELATION TO
SOVEREIGN GRACE

"By grace are ye saved. . . ."—Eph. 2:8

We must now consider an important matter in which there may easily be misapprehension and false conclusion. At first hearing, it may be thought that emphasizing the sovereignty of Christ in relation to the terms of salvation nullifies the true doctrine of *grace* and implies that human works avail in the securing of eternal life. But a little careful thought and a proper perspective will rectify such a misconception. Far be the thought that legality saves. Such a suggestion must be emphatically disavowed. It is ever "the grace of God that bringeth salvation" (Titus 2:11), and the sinner is saved on the ground of sovereign grace and grace alone. The whole operation, from its Alpha to its Omega, is of the unmerited favor of God without even a scintilla of human merit. It is ever God who takes the initiative and by His sovereign work in the human heart and will enables an exercise of saving faith. The old-time problem of reconciling divine sovereignty with human volition is not the subject of our consideration, nor does it fundamentally affect our theme.

It must be stressed, however, that the grace of God ever leads the believing heart to the exalted Lord and alone enables the soul to make Jesus King. The Holy Spirit's one function and delight is to glorify the risen Lord. Where is boasting then? Where is human merit? It is excluded. Salvation (which is receiving Christ as Lord) is all "by grace ... through faith, *not of works*." That a rebel sinner should be privileged ever to become a loyal saint is all of divine grace and mercy. That he who consented to, and even acclaimed, the crucifixion of the Son of God should ever find it possible to proclaim His coronation is nothing less than a miracle of sovereign grace. That an insurgent sinner by an act of reception (John 1:12) should be given the authority to become a child of God is all of grace—free, sovereign, matchless grace! To relate the whole experience of salvation, from initial reception to the fullest realization, is only to "tell the story—saved by grace." Even in practical sanctification and the performance of good works which evidence salvation, there is no thought of human merit. Are we not "*his* workmanship, created in Christ Jesus unto good works"? It is grace which enables the believer to be filled with the Spirit. Let it be affirmed dogmatically that it is grace which leads the soul to bow to His sovereignty. Personal salvation is not a meritorious effort (as some may think) to *make Christ Lord* of the life. It is the reception of Him who is *the Lord* in submissive faith, and such subsequent, moment-by-moment yielding of all to His sway as will *demonstrate* His sovereignty in and through a sanctified personality.

The gospel of THY GRACE my stubborn heart has won.

It is possible, however, to receive the grace of God in vain.

CHAPTER VII

HIS SOVEREIGNTY
IN RELATION TO
THE BODY

"The head of every man is Christ."—I
Cor. 11:3

It is important to consider the similes
which the Holy Spirit employs to exem-
plify the vital truth of the believer's
union with the risen Lord and to notice
how each emphasizes divine rulership as
the necessary corollary of faith. Is not every believer introduced into membership
of the body of Christ? And does it not
follow that the very constitution of such
union implies an acknowledgment of Him
who is the head? So far as the members
of this body are concerned, "the head of
every man is Christ" (I Cor. 16:3). Is He
not "head over all things to the church,

which is his body"? (Eph. 1:22-23)

In that delightful little booklet *A Prince and a Saviour*, the author illustrates this truth from the Old Testament as follows:

> Jephthah the Gileadite was a mighty man of valour, one of God's strong men, but there was a stain on his birth, so his brothers cast him out of the family and he had to flee to Tob. Years after, the brothers got into bondage to the Ammonites, who cruelly oppressed them. Then they remembered Jephthah, the mighty man, and sent to him to come and deliver them. Now Jephthah rightly complained: "Did not ye hate me and expel me out of my father's house? And why are ye come unto me now when ye are in distress?" But the people urged him to come. Then he replied: "If I come and save you, shall I be your Head?" This is what Christ says: "If I am to be Saviour, I must be Prince, Lord, Head of you and your Life!!"

How often the Holy Spirit likens union with Christ to the highest and most sacred of all earthly unions—the marriage tie. In this connection Paul says clearly: "I speak concerning Christ and the church" (Eph. 5:32). There is ample New Testament authority for regarding the first man Adam as a type of Christ, and the "help-meet" for him as a type of the Church. In Romans 7:4, Paul refers to believers as "married . . . to him who is raised from the dead, that we should bring forth fruit unto God." How significant, therefore, is the word of Eph. 5:23: "The husband is the head of the wife, even as Christ is the *head* of the church."

All true believers are joined to the risen Lord, one spirit. This is the "Body of Christ." It is not the "body of Jesus." The latter was His earthly body, while the former is a spiritual organism in which He *now* resides on the earth. In this connection a suggestive contrast is noticeable in Luke 25:52, and 24:2, concerning the Saviour's body. In the former reference, Joseph of Arimathaea begs "the body of Jesus." After the resurrection, the Holy Spirit records a few verses later that those who came to the sepulchre with their spices "found not the body of the Lord Jesus." We therefore never read in the Epistles of the "body of Jesus." Even in speaking of the offered body, the writer of the Hebrews letter designates that precious temple as the "body of Jesus *Christ*."

Does it not follow logically, then, that regeneration, or believing *into* Christ, and thus becoming a living member of His body and a partaker of His life, involves a submissive consent to His headship? Members of a headless body are dead. Further, a body with many heads is a monstrosity. Every believer is necessarily joined to the one Head. Manifestly, therefore, the one and only basis of genuine union with Christ is *subjection* to His headship (Eph. 5:24). To speak of possessing the Holy Spirit and yet refusing the Lordship of the One to whom He witnesses is obviously a paradox. "The Holy Spirit was not given, for Jesus was not yet glorified." Therein lies a vital principle as well as a historic fact. The Holy Spirit indwells the believing sinner to one supreme end, that Jesus may be glorified as Lord. Salvation is not something received *from* Christ, but is something found *in* Christ.

CHAPTER VIII

HIS SOVEREIGNTY
IN RELATION TO
DEFECTIVE CONSECRATION

"Ye were the servants of sin.... now being made free from sin."—Rom. 6: 20-22

An important question arises here, in which there is need for clear spiritual perspective. If salvation is nothing less than an acknowledgment of Christ's sovereignty, what of the backslider or carnal Christian? Clearly, every true believer does not *fully* respond to the implications of His Lordship. Indeed, where is the child of God who perfectly allows the Holy Spirit to work it out in every detail of life? Only One has ever trod the soil of earth who could say: "I do always those things which please the

Father" (John 8:29). Does such faulty discipleship imply that eternal life is not possessed, and that such an one was never truly born again? Surely not! For who then could be saved? At best we are only "unprofitable servants." Thank God, salvation is not dependent upon the measure of the believer's faithfulness, but upon the faithfulness of God in the provision of a perfect Saviour, and the sinner's reception of Him as his righteousness.

But it must be stated with equal clarity that a deliberate continuance in sin contradicts the nature of true faith and is never anticipated in the divine scheme. Liberty is not licence. Of course, it must be sadly admitted that backsliding and carnality are realities of Christian experience, but the important emphasis we are stressing has not to do with contingencies subsequent to conversion, but rather the initial act of believing by which the sinner consents to a new principle of sovereignty. Until the end of the journey there will be those who follow "afar off," even though there is provision in Christ for *full* salvation. The point is that every backslider or carnal Christian must initially have acknowledged the Lordship of Christ in heart faith. It is only the natural (or unregenerate) man who says, "I *will not* have this Man to *reign* over me." If the believer fails to respond as fully as he ought to this new mastery, his weakness and failure does not nullify the *principle* to which he originally gave the consent of his will by divine grace.

There is apparently so much misunderstanding on this point that it is important to state the matter clearly. Let it therefore be reaffirmed with conviction that the believer's salvation and security does not depend upon his perfect response to all that the sovereignty of Christ means in practical life. Such would, indeed, be a gospel of legalism. The practicing of Christ's Lordship is rather the *outcome or evidence* of the fact that His sovereignty has been initially recognized. The acknowledgment of His right to reign is the first step into life. Then, as the Lord is given the place of supremacy in heart and life, by a willing consent and unreserved surrender day by day, so all that His sovereignty means finds a practical outworking. Only thus can a believer "possess his possessions" in Christ and turn the facts of faith into factors of experience. It has been well said that "joy is the flag which is flown from the castle of the heart when the King is in residence."

Further, it is the experience of almost every believer that spiritual history is marked by very definite post-conviction crises, some of which appear to be almost more real than conversion itself. This is usually the arrival of the soul at a new place of "surrender," sometimes referred to as "full consecration." It is a fresh willingness to yield *fully* to the Lord. It is the removal of all known barriers to wholehearted obedience, and a full consent to the death of the self life. Most Christians can testify to such a crisis. But again, we must not confuse the issue. Whether consecration be partial or full, post-conversion developments in no way negate the vital principle that *His sovereignty is necessary to salvation.* A willingness for full surrender is not to be confused with the soul's initial amen to the Lordship of Christ, as though such surrender introduces a new principle of sovereignty as distinct from that which commences to operate at conversion. We have established the fact that regeneration itself implies a new creation life in which Christ is *Lord.* Any subsequent experience of surrender is but a fresh point of willingness to allow the Holy Spirit to *work out* that new principle of life. The crisis is followed by the process, but each relates to His Lordship. The first is consent to the new sovereignty in principle; subsequent crises relate to His sovereignty in practice. This is the "obedience of faith."

In Acts 5:14, we discern a contradiction in the words of Peter when he said: "Not so, *Lord.*" Obviously, the words "not so" or the word "Lord" must be dropped. A friend says: "I spent two hours with a lady over these words, and then I wrote them down in the margin of her Bible at the bottom of the page. I handed her the Bible and the pencil and said: 'The time has come for you to make the decision. Are you going to score out the words "not so" or the word "Lord"?' There was a great struggle, and through tears she crossed out the words 'not so.' I said: 'What do you have left?' and she said: 'The Lord.' Is not 'the Lord' enough?"

This should be the normal result of the new life and is the place of complete yielding to which the Holy Spirit would lead every believer.

It was not without reason that, in the midst of deep thought along this line, the writer received a significant letter from a young fellow which read as follows:

Can I come to Christ and trust Him without taking Him as Lord of all my life?—without promising to obey all that He may ask me to perform? In other words, can I trust Him, without any obligation, in order to be justified? Can I claim Christ as my Saviour without being willing at that time to part with any pet sin? Having read some messages on the way of life, I gather that a sinner can claim Christ as Saviour, and then in the knowledge of being justified from the guilt of sin—past, present and future—he will endeavour of his own will to crown Christ as King.

What was the correct answer to that inquiry? The reply was sympathetically direct. It emphasized the danger of any kind of believism which leaves the will ungoverned, the heart unchanged, and the spirit unquickened. It would seem obvious that here was a young man who had been deceived by an inadequate, if not erroneous, message. How could it be countenanced for a moment that true faith in Christ permits a loophole for continuance in sin? "Can I claim Christ as my Saviour without being willing to part with any pet sin?" The scriptural answer is clear: "When ye were the servants of sin, ye were free from righteousness. What fruit had ye then in those things *whereof ye are now ashamed*? For the end of those things is in death. But *now* being made free from sin, and *become* servants to God, ye have your *fruit unto holiness*, and the end everlasting life" (Rom. 6:20-22).

The young man's question is asked in scriptural language in this same chapter: "Shall we *continue in sin* that grace may abound?" (vs. 1). There is only one answer, plain and emphatic: "God forbid!" Faith which allows a continuance in sin is but a paradox. While in the blessed decree of grace there is unfailing provision for the true child of God who falls into sin, let us never be tempted into the hazardous idea that believing "unto the saving of the soul" can sanction any kind of secret, rebellious resolve. To profess conversion and then deliberately continue in some phase of disobedience *without misgiving or compunction* is to destroy true evidence of life.

As we have seen already, salvation is a heart consent to divine Lordship as a new principle of life. Apart from this, wherein lies its value? Of course, a lapse of disobedience in the believer, through loss of communion with the heavenly Father, is sadly possible. Indeed, which of us can claim exemption from spiritual failure? (see I John 1:7). But blessed be God for His wonderful provision, "If we confess our sins, he is faithful and just to forgive us our sins, and to cleanse us from all unrighteousness" (I John 1:9). But let it be engraven deeply in every mind and heart that true faith never embodies a licence to *go on sinning*, nor does it know any reserve in the matter of allegiance.

The will of God, in its normal outworkings for the believer, is expressed in the words "that ye *sin not*" (I John 2:1). The Saviour's command to the woman taken in adultery was, "Go and sin no more." Having heard "no condemnation" (John 8:2), she is exhorted to live according to that privilege. Let us not separate the "no more" of salvation (Heb. 8:12) from the "no more" of sanctification (John 8:2). When faith is stripped of its normal compulsions, and the sinner desires a salvation which is compatible with a program of self-pleasing, fleshly indulgence, and worldliness, then such a "faith" bears the inevitable brand of counterfeit.

Why did another young man—the rich young ruler—turn sorrowfully away from the Lord? He believed in Him in the sense of confidence in the truth of His message, but the crucial issue had to do with His government. He refused the sovereignty of Christ in the matter of his possessions, and thus "went away sorrowful" (Luke 18:23). The evidence of love to Christ is unswerving obedience to His will and words. Conversion, resulting in the gift of the Holy Spirit, is nothing less than a deliberate consent to *obey* (Acts 5:32).

What sort of spiritual experience can be behind the oft-repeated argument for worldliness, "I can take Christ with me to these places." Never! He does not *follow*. He *leads* as *Lord*. When the Saviour had washed the disciples' feet, *He* said unto them: "Ye call me master and Lord: and ye say well; for so I am" (John 13:13). But it is significant that in the next sentence He reverses the order and says: "If I then, your *Lord* and master. . . ." His sovereignty *must* come first, and forms the true basis of effective *service*.

CHAPTER IX

HIS SOVEREIGNTY
IN RELATION TO
THE GOSPEL

"If Christ be not risen, then is our preaching vain, and your faith is also vain."—
I Cor. 15:14

What Is the Gospel?

What is the real gospel of the New Testament with which the Lord's ambassadors have been entrusted? The gospel that Paul loved to call "my gospel" was essentially the gospel of the risen and ascended *Lord*. This is abundantly clear in the classic utterance of I Cor. 15. In a matter of fourteen words, he lays the vital and all-imperative foundation of Calvary's atoning sacrifice:

Christ died for our sins according to the scriptures; and that he was buried . . ." (vss. 3-4)

Then, in a tremendous and weighty

declaration extending over seventeen verses, he emphasizes the glorious fact of the *resurrection*. This, says he, is "the gospel which I preached unto you." It is essentially the gospel of the crucified and *risen Christ*. This is something more than the *living* Christ. He lived on earth as the Son of Man, and the rationalistic critic will thus speak of the living Christ. But the New Testament gospel concerns and exalts the *risen* Christ. Such an evangel includes, by presupposition, His precious atoning death as the one and only basis of God's dealings with men. "I am he that liveth and was dead, and am alive again for evermore."

This is the gospel of our salvation, and while we must constantly stand with feet unshod and hearts bowed on the hill outside the city wall, the message we preach is one of glorious triumph and resurrection life. But of this, more later.

The writer was very impressed recently to discover that nowhere in the New Testament is the saviourhood of Christ referred to without an accompanying allusion, either directly or indirectly, to *His resurrection and His Godhead*. Mary rejoices in "*God* my Saviour." Such expressions as "*God* my Saviour," "Christ the Saviour," "A Prince and a Saviour," "The Lord Jesus Christ our Saviour," "Our Lord and Saviour" are indeed significant. It is possible to speak almost glibly about "our Saviour," but let it never be forgotten that no man can say Jesus is Lord, but by the Holy Spirit (I Cor. 12:3). Of course, the emphasis here is not on the *saying*. It is more than mere acknowledgment, for the word is equally clear that "not every one that *saith*, . . . Lord, Lord, shall enter . . . but he that *doeth* . . . " (Matt. 7:21-22).

The Message of the Early Church

It is impossible to read, even cursorily, the early chapters of the Acts without noticing the outstanding emphasis of the gospel preached by the early church. It was the transcendent message of the resurrected LORD. Nor did they merely preach the resurrection as a doctrine, but rather the Person of Him who forever is "declared to be the Son of God with power, . . . by the resurrection from the dead" (Rom. 1:4). Listen to Peter's pronouncement on the Day of Pentecost:

Ye men of Israel, hear these words;
Jesus of Nazareth, a man approved of
God among you by miracles and wonders and signs, which God did by him
in the midst of you, as ye yourselves also
know: him, being delivered by the de-
terminate counsel and foreknowledge of
God, ye have taken, and by wicked hands
have crucified and slain; whom God
hath raised up, having loosed the pains
of death: because it was not possible
that he should be holden of it. (Acts
2:22-24)

Again, in verses 32-36:

This Jesus hath God raised up, whereof we all are witnesses. Therefore being
by the right hand of God exalted, and
having received of the Father the promise
of the Holy Ghost, he hath shed forth
this, which ye now see and hear. For
David is not ascended into the heavens:
but he saith himself, The Lord said unto
my Lord, Sit thou on my right hand,
until I make thy foes thy footstool. Therefore let all the house of Israel know assuredly, that God hath made *that same
Jesus, whom ye have crucified, both Lord
and Christ.*

This was the message which the Holy
Spirit applied in terrific conviction to the

conscience of the hearers. "They were pricked in their heart" and cried, "What shall we do?" Notice there was no frantic effort to produce some kind of expression of faith on the part of reluctant hearers. The spiritual impact of the resurrection message is so specific that they are tremendously concerned to know what the next step should be! Peter, in no uncertain way, calls them to repentance (see later chapter). It has ever been, and ever will be, the gospel of the risen and exalted Lord that stirs the souls of men, convicts of spiritual bankruptcy, and draws men to God.

Again, in Acts 3, with a new-born courage born of Pentecost, Peter boldly declares that the "Holy One and the Just," whom they had denied, was the "Prince of life, whom God had raised from the dead." By "his name, and faith in his name," a lame man had miraculously been made strong. Down through the ages since, men who are lamed by sin have found spiritual healing through the gospel of resurrection life.

Further (vs. 19), the preaching of the risen Lord was marvelously effective:

> The multitude of them that believed were of one heart and one soul . . . and with great power gave the apostles witness of the RESURRECTION of the Lord Jesus: and great grace was upon them all. (Acts 4:32-33)

In Peter's sermon to the Gentile hearers recorded in chapter 10, we read in verse 36 that the sovereignty of the risen Christ is his predominant theme. It is certain that, with the Apostle Paul, Peter would rather speak five words with understanding than ten thousand words unintelligibly (I Cor. 14:19). In his wonderful sermon there is a sentence of five words which encompasses all the blessings and implications of the gospel message. "He is Lord of all" (vs. 36). This was Jesus of Nazareth, anointed with the Holy Ghost, continually evidencing His sovereignty, who went about doing good, whom they slew and hanged on a tree. "Him God hath raised up the third day and shewed him openly" (vss. 39-40). Notice again the effect of this preaching. "While Peter yet spake these words, the Holy Ghost fell on all them which heard the word" (vs. 44).

Passing on to Acts 17, we read of Paul

establishing a church at Thessalonica. Observe the basis of his appeal and the spiritual philosophy of his reasonings with them "out of the scriptures" (vs. 2). He openly alleges that the Man who was nailed in weakness to a Roman gibbet is the risen Man in the glory at God's right hand. "This Jesus, whom I preach unto you, is Christ" (vs. 3).

One Gospel Only

Reference may profitably be made at this stage to the distinction often made between the gospel of the grace of God and the gospel of the kingdom. A danger which continually besets the gospel preacher is the tendency to over-emphasize one side of divine truth at the expense of another.

This practice on the part of some Bible interpreters has resulted in forfeiting proper scriptural perspective.

What is the gospel of God's grace but the gospel of HIS sovereignty? And wherein lies the vital efficacy of the gospel of grace unless it relates to *His king-*

dom and leads the individual soul to an acknowledgment of His sovereignty?

At the same time, there is no controversy whatever in the matter of *distinct dispensational aspects* of the gospel, and no doubt this is the intention of these segregations of the evangel according to its varying titles in the Word. But is it not important to guard against the possibility of such unbalanced distinctions that we minimize the one and only objective of grace, i.e., *His sovereignty?* It is earnestly affirmed that there is *only one gospel* in the Scriptures, and this supremely unique evangel must of necessity result, at all times and to whomsoever declared, in the enthronement of the Lord Jesus. Whether it has to do with the kingdom in mystery in this age, or the kingdom in manifestation in the golden age to come, it is vitally of one and the same substance—the gospel of His sovereignty.

Notice, further, how precise the Holy Spirit is in the manifold designations by which He describes this gospel. Though many appellations are used, it is significant that each one conveys the essential truth of the resurrection and the Godhead. Here are some:

> "The Gospel of *Jesus Christ*" (Mark 1:1).
> "The Gospel of the Grace of *God*" (Acts 20:24).
> "The Gospel of *God*" (Romans 1:1).
> "The Gospel of *Christ*" (Romans 1:16).
> "The Gospel of the *Glory of Christ*" (II Cor. 4:4 RV).
> "The Gospel of our *Lord* Jesus Christ" (II Thess. 1:8).
> "*Christ's* Gospel" (II Cor. 2:12).

All these link grace to glory, and insist that the gospel of His love is inseparable from His preeminence. In the phraseology of our popular twentieth century Christian religion, we are forced to observe a sad and striking contrast. Much is heard today of the "gospel of Jesus," the "Jesus of history," the "social gospel," etc. Indeed, these seem to be the popular slogans of Christendom in these days of apostasy and spiritual decline. The Gospel entrusted to the King's ambassadors is never called "the gospel of Jesus." This evangel bears all the dynamic and dignity of the throne of God. Its demands cause the sinner to bow in humble submission, worship, and obedience before the exalted One who fills heaven with His glory! It is "the Gospel of the glory" (II Cor. 4:4, RV). This is "the gospel of your salvation." While believers must refuse bondage to mere phraseology, it is felt that care should be exercised when alluding to the Saviour to give Him His title as "*Lord*," using such Scripture designations as "The Lord Jesus," "The Lord Jesus Christ," "The Lord Christ," "Christ the Lord," or just "The Lord."

Of course, there are devoted believers who, in conversation and in preaching make constant reference to the Saviour as "Jesus." It is not suggested that any derogation of His Lordship or majesty is either introduced or resultant. It will be agreed, however, that it is not erring on the side of reverence and worship to give Him the glory due unto Him as we take that precious name upon our lips.

The Preacher's Theme

The paramount theme of the gospel preacher is therefore the death, resurrection, ascension and return of our Lord Jesus Christ, and the divine objective to be realized through His redemptive work. This can be nothing less than the proclamation of His sovereignty in relation to the redemption of men. "For to this end, Christ both died, and rose, and revived, that he might be Lord both of the dead and of the living" (Rom. 14:9).

It is the "gospel of the glory of Christ" (II Cor. 4:4—RV). Any "gospel," however orthodox in its presentation, which falls short of the resurrection, either expressly or by implication, is not the true gospel of salvation. Of course, every true preacher of the gospel rejoices in the glorious fact that He who died also *rose again and is alive to die no more.* This fact is undoubtedly assumed or implied in every faithful gospel message. There is a subtle danger, however, which needs to be honestly faced and overcome. It is the tendency to declare the Saviour's death on the Cross for sinners, and *that alone!* Blessed and glorious as this truth is, it is not a complete gospel, and may even be the means of counterfeit results. While the essential basis of the true

gospel appeal must ever be "Christ crucified," it must never leave the hearers
with a "crucified Christ." The plain fact
is that *Christ on the Cross* can save no-
body. He was "crucified in weakness."
The atoning sacrifice of Calvary is ever
the eternal basis of salvation, but it is
the *risen* Lord, and He alone, who saves.

May it not be that much of the disappointment accruing from our gospel testimony could be traced primarily to the
inadequacy of the message preached?
The gospel is not a message of death, but
of life, life in the risen Lord, and that only
because He died for sinners. A dead
Christ, or a crucifix, can only be a symbol
of darkness and despair. How often a test
question is put to a seeking soul: "Do you
believe that Jesus *died* for you?" "Oh,
yes." "Then you are saved." But *is* that
adequate? Such a belief may lead a soul
only out of one hiding place into another.
As we have seen already, true faith relates to the crucified and risen Lord as
a Person, and is not merely the acceptance of *facts.*

Of course, the Word of God is not
bound, nor is the Holy Spirit necessarily

89

circumscribed by the limitations of the message or the messenger. Indeed, such a message has often been blessed of God to the salvation of souls. Thank God, true conversion is *spiritual revelation*, and may be granted by the Holy Spirit through the most inadequate agency. Light may enter the soul through an individual sentence, or just a word, or even without the preacher's message at all! God in His sovereignty will have mercy upon whom He will have mercy, and so far as the messenger is concerned, more may depend upon his personal sanctification as a vessel than upon his actual emphasis or method in presenting the Gospel.

It is not suggested for a moment that every aspect of gospel truth can (or should) be incorporated into one message. Such would be well-nigh an impossibility, but it is suggested the *resurrected Christ* is the One whom we preach, and that the sovereignty of the risen Lord is the dominating principle forming the background of every true evangelistic appeal.

While Calvary must ever be supreme

in the message, it should be remembered that the intrinsic value of the blood of Christ and His atoning sacrifice is primarily *Godward*, and it is the resurrection of the One who hung there which attests and secures its undying significance to needy sinners. The gospel of the glory is essentially the gospel of the Cross. It is *the Lamb* who is "in the midst of the throne." It is impossible to preach the gospel of His sovereignty without recognizing the Cross as fundamentally basic and central. But "if Christ be not raised, ye are yet in your sins and your faith is vain."

The Cross and the Crown cannot be logically separated. In the wonderful types and shadows of the Old Testament, all of which are concerning Jesus as the crucified and risen *Lord*, the central fact of the atonement is prominent. See how holy men of God prophesied not only of His sufferings, but also of the *glory* that should follow. The Cross and the glory are inseparable. As in the case of Thomas, an adequate vision of the nail-pierced hands and feet must ever lead to the worshipful exclamation, *"My Lord and my God!*" There the doubter found an answer to all his fears and questionings. Multitudes since have found the same blessings in the same way. The gospel of the resurrection has never lost its power.

Thus, the Holy Spirit witnesses to the saving power of the risen Lord. The preacher's theme is still the same today. It is not only the *doctrine* of the atoning sacrifice of Calvary, but the inseparable corollary that He "'rose again on the third day according to the scriptures" (I Cor. 15:4). In full compatability with this all-embracing theme, the Apostle sums up his own main emphasis and that of all divinely ordained ambassadors. "We preach not ourselves, but Christ Jesus the Lord" (II Cor. 4:5). The Revised Version is more accurate and very significant in the change of one little word: "Christ Jesus *as* Lord." Is it not clearly conclusive that preaching the saviourhood of Christ is synonymous with the proclamation of His Lordship?

Further, let the preacher never forget that his own personal and experimental union with Christ in death and resurrection can alone qualify him for such a ministry. *It takes a crucified and risen Christian to effectually preach a crucified and risen Christ.* It involves the subjective outworking of the Cross in practical experience day by day, for manifestly there can be no evincing or resurrection life apart from death. *His* death, yes, but also that of every believer. Is it not only as he mortifies that which is of the natural that he can share the life of the heavenlies? No flesh can glory in that realm. To see Him is to fall at His feet as one dead. Surely a full and glad consent to His sovereignty is the vital need of the church of God today! Efficiency of administration or orthodoxy of message—important as these may be—are not synonymous with spiritual effectiveness nor must they be allowed to supplant the vital essential of a corporate and individual "Amen" to *His preeminence.*

Dr. Scofield once said:

I shall never forget when a passage in Joshua concerning the Captain of the Lord's host came home to me. I had begun to take a certain pleasure or pride, far more than I suspected, in being the pastor of a growing and working Church. I was not very conscious of it, but there was a kind of complacency in beginning to be talked about a little. And then I came across the passage in Joshua, and do you know what I did? I resigned my pastorate immediately—not to the Church; I said not a word to the Church about it for two years, but I said to the Lord: "I have been figuring around before these people as Captain of the Lord's host. Now I resign. Be Thou Captain." And from that day until the day I regretfully laid that pastorate down, I never felt an hour's burden of it.

Familiar Texts

It has recently come home with conviction to the writer that many of the best-loved and most-used texts employed in our gospel messages embody in themselves the relationship of sovereignty to salvation. It was a humiliating realization that although this truth had been projecting with divinely arranged prominence in texts constantly quoted, yet its vital significance had never really registered in mind and heart.

Take the familiar word in John 1:12, for instance: "But as many as received *him*, to them gave he power to become the children of God. . . ." Why does the Holy Spirit employ the personal pronoun "Him" in this case? Is it not to stress the glory and majesty of the Person who is to be received? Who is this glorious One whose entrance into the heart constitutes the right to membership of God's family? He is described in verses 1-2:

> In the beginning was the Word, and the Word was with God, and the Word *was* God. The same was in the beginning with God.

Wonder of wonders! Regeneration is lifted to its highest pinnacle of dignity and consequence here. It is nothing less than God himself dwelling within a human heart. This One who is received for salvation is God the eternal Word (vss. 1-2), the Almighty Creator (vs. 3), the Source of Light and Life (vs. 4). This is our "Lord and Saviour, Jesus Christ."

> Behold, I stand at the door, and knock: if any man hear my voice, and open the door, I will come in to him, and will sup with him, and he with me. (Rev. 3:20)

What lovelier words could express the Saviour's desire and promise concerning His incoming? But how often an inadequate conception of its real significance is suggested in our very phraseology! We speak of Jesus standing at the door and seeking admission. So easily we convey the impression—quite unconsciously—that the Lord of glory is courting a favor as He looks for a heart that is willing to respond. How utterly incongruous and irreverent! Let us turn back a page or two, and then stand with awe and reverence in the august presence of this glorious Person who stands at the door of the Church that bears His name! Who is He? John says:

> When I saw *him*, I fell at his feet as dead. And he laid his right hand upon me, saying unto me, Fear not; I am the first and the last. *I am he that liveth, and was dead*; and behold, I am alive for evermore, amen; and have the keys of hell and of death. (Rev. 1:17-18)

Yes, He is the Alpha and Omega, the Almighty, the Head of the Church (read the glorious description of Him in verses 13-16). Little wonder that John, looking upon His majesty, fell at His feet like one dead! He is the mighty Conqueror of death and Hades, and the One who holds the keys of triumph forever. Yet, this is He who deigns to make a human heart His palace, and actually condescends to knock for admission. Yes, it is Jesus at the door, but it is the *Lord* Jesus. God forbid that we should ever be unmindful of His dignity and majesty!

> That if thou shalt confess with thy mouth the Lord Jesus, and shalt believe in thine heart that God hath raised him from the dead, thou shalt be saved. (Rom. 10:9)

Perhaps no other verse so clearly states the condition of salvation as this. What are the terms? First, confessing "Jesus *as Lord.*" Here, as clearly as language can pronounce it, the saviourhood of Christ is coupled with His sovereignty. He is confessed as Lord. Second, it is believing in the heart "that God hath *raised him* from the dead." It will be seen at once that such a belief extends far beyond a mere assent to the doctrine of Calvary. Here, the blessed

Saviour who eternally atoned for sin, is attested as the *risen One*, and belief in the heart is linked with Him as the ascended Lord. "God hath exalted him to be a prince and a Saviour." As such, He must be believed in (or received) "unto salvation."

For the wages of sin is death; but the gift of God is eternal life through [Gr.: *in*] Jesus Christ our Lord. (Rom. 6:23)

Here, again, eternal life is in and through Jesus Christ our Lord. There is a triple completeness in this title which presents the risen One as Saviour, King, and Lord. As such, He is the giver of eternal life. Salvation belongeth unto the Lord. Life is found through union with Him who is the Lord of life.

But these are written, that ye might believe that Jesus is the Christ, the Son of God; and that believing ye might have life through his name. (John 20:31)

And as Moses lifted up the serpent in the wilderness, even so must the Son of man be lifted up: that whosoever believeth in him should not perish, but have eternal life. (John 3:14-15)

Here the beautiful type of the serpent

in the wilderness is very significant. As the bitten Israelites looked to the serpent on the pole for healing, so belief in the "lifted up" One brings eternal life to the sin-cursed sinner. But not only was our Substitute "lifted up" to die. He was also lifted up into glory by the power of God. While it is blessedly true that "there is life in a look at the crucified One," it is important to realize that it is the risen One who alone can impart resurrection life, *though* (let it again be said) *solely on the basis of His atoning death*. It is the Risen One who says, "Look unto Me."

> "Lifted up" was He to die,
> "It is finished," was His cry;
> Now in Heaven EXALTED HIGH,
> Hallelujah, what a Saviour!

Eternal life is received by believing in the *Son of God*.

> He that believeth on the Son hath everlasting life: and he that believeth not the Son shall not see life; but the wrath of God abideth on him. (John 3:36)
> And this is the record, that God hath given to us eternal life; and this life is *in* his Son. He that hath the Son hath life; and he that hath not the Son of God

99

hath not life. These things have I written unto you that believe on the name of the Son of God; that ye may know that ye have eternal life, and that ye may believe on the name of the Son of God. (I John 5:11-13)

This is life eternal, that they might know thee, *the only true God*, and Jesus Christ, whom thou hast sent. (John 17:3)

Come unto me, all ye that labour and are heavy laden, and I will give you rest. (Matt. 11:28)

Is there any sweeter gospel invitation than this? "Come unto *me!*" Yes, "Jesus is tenderly calling," but who is this glorious Rest-Giver? It is well that gospel preachers should note the previous verse:

All things are delivered unto me of my Father: and no man knoweth the Son, but the Father; neither knoweth any man the Father, save the Son, and *he* to whomsoever the Son will reveal him. (Matt. 11:27)

It is the Son who gives rest! He who is One with the Father, sharing His counsels, and who alone can reveal Him. He is not only the meek and lowly one, but the exalted Prince of Glory. Let us beware of too cheap a conception of "coming to Jesus." Such coming manifestly involves a heart subjection to His will, while this glorious rest of soul is promised only to those who take His yoke upon them (vs. 29).

> Take my yoke upon you, and learn of me; for I am meek and lowly in heart: and ye shall find rest unto your souls.
> Be it known unto you therefore, men and brethren, that through this man is preached unto you the forgiveness of sins. (Acts 13:38)

Who is this Man through whom forgiveness is preached and by whom all who believe are justified? The question is answered in the previous verse (37). It is He *whom God raised again* and who saw no corruption. This Man is the blessed Pardoner and Justifier of sinners.

Limited space forbids quotation of many other well-known gospel texts. Each enforces the same great truth. Justification is "in the name of the Lord Jesus" (I Cor. 6:11). True believers, constituting the Church of God, are "added to the Lord" (Acts 5:14). "The Lord knoweth them that are his" (II Tim. 2:19). The church is a spiritual building, which grows "unto a holy temple in the Lord" (Eph. 2:21). "Whether we live or die, we are the Lord's" (Rom. 14:8).

In view of this clearly defined emphasis, is there not a very real danger of placing an unscriptural gap between the *saviourhood of Jesus* and the *sovereignty of Christ*? Such is an illogical distinction which can never be recognized by the Holy Spirit. In the realm of spiritual realities, there is no such thing as *receiving His saviourhood* while *refusing His Lordship*. How often acceptance of Christ as *Lord* is regarded as a post-conversion decision! Truly a sinking sinner needs a Saviour first, but obviously He cannot be received as Saviour while refused as Lord. He cannot be the one without the other. Everything for time and eternity hangs upon the answer of the heart to our Lord's own question, "Whom say ye that I am?" "What think ye of Christ? *Whose Son is he?*" True conversion is a spiritual apprehension of *who He is*—the sovereign Lord. This produces a heart revelation which must, in its very nature, result in a heart revolution.

A believer had the words "Christ Is Lord" inscribed on the face of his watch. There are twelve letters in that phrase, and each represented an hour. When he looked at his watch to ascertain the time, he would say to himself, "Well, Christ is Lord, whatever the time."

CHAPTER X

HIS SOVEREIGNTY
IN RELATION TO
THE CHRISTMAS MESSAGE

"Glory to God in the highest, and on earth peace, good-will toward men."
—Luke 2:14

This glorious gospel of divine sovereignty is very definitely proclaimed in the opening expression of good tidings on the first Christmas Day. In due time the promised Saviour had come. Deity combined with dust, and a holy Babe was born in Bethlehem. This was the God-Man. The shepherds watching their flocks by night were suddenly startled by the appearance of the angel of the Lord, while the nocturnal gloom was dispelled by the effulgence of heavenly glory. Such a miracle was worthy of the occasion.

> And the angel said unto them, Fear not: for behold, I bring you good tidings of great joy, which shall be to all people. For unto you is born this day, in the city of David, a Saviour, which is Christ the Lord. (Luke 2:10-11)

Note the identity of the Babe. He is the "Saviour who is Christ the *Lord*." Thus, the very first gospel message of the Christian era strikes the keynote of true evangelism. Notice again:

> And suddenly there was with the angel a multitude of the heavenly host praising God, and saying, Glory to God in the highest, and on earth peace, good-will toward men. (Luke 2:13-14)

It is significant that the very first words uttered by the multitude of the heavenly host should stress primarily the *glory of God* rather than man's pardon, salvation and happiness, though these are the blessed fruits of faith. Glory to God in the highest—that is the supreme objective of this evangel. The God whose name has been dishonored and whose glory has been traduced by sin may now be glorified in the hearts of those who have rebelled against Him. Glorious news, indeed! Then follows the logical sequence of blessing: "Peace on earth."

Peace on earth! Is not the very phrase much like a mockery as we behold the troubled seas of human affairs today? Where is this "peace on earth" promised so long ago? It must be admitted that the Saviour's first advent, nearly two millenniums ago, was accompanied by the promise, but where is it? Has the promise failed, or the scheme miscarried? Across the centuries since then men have looked in vain and striven towards the Golden Age of universal tranquillity, but it would seem that we were never more remote from its realization than we are today! With "wars and rumours of wars," the world is a boiling cauldron of unrest, and "men's hearts are failing them for fear." "Peace on earth!" says the skeptic ironically. "Your Saviour has come and gone; your Christianity is a failure; two thousand years of our Gospel has failed in its objective. It is a farce, and not a force!"

Here is a challenge! How are we to answer it? Has Christianity failed? Is the divine purpose annulled? Has the Gospel of the first Christmas Day become ineffective? The secret, of course, is found in an adequate conception of the principle of sovereignty upon which the divine promises are fulfilled. Why is there no peace on earth among the nations? The answer is in the text:

GLORY TO GOD in the Highest. . . .

This is more than an ascription of praise to the Highest; it is at the same time a pronouncement of *peace terms* to a rebellious world. It proclaims the sovereignty of Christ as conditional. The fundamental explanation of world unrest today is the fact that God's *condition of peace* has never yet been fulfilled by man. Alas, God has never yet been given the glory. He has been shut out of the affairs of men and nations throughout this evil age. Man has endeavored to govern his own affairs with the result that world chaos reigns and civilization is well-nigh shipwrecked.

But will the promise of peace on earth *never* be realized? Yes, thank God, in the coming age of His sovereignty, when

He sits upon the throne of universal sway, there shall be peace on earth. "Nations shall not learn war any more" (Isa. 2:4), and "The earth shall be full of the knowledge of the Lord as the waters cover the sea" (Isa. 11:9). In that wonderful day, as men give universal glory to God, there will be universal peace. The God-Man will come into His rightful place as the "blessed and only Potentate, King of kings, and Lord of lords" (I Tim. 6:15). Not until that glorious age can there be any permanent solution of the intricate problems which baffle our statesmen today.

It is a simple matter of cause and effect. Like the law of the Medes and Persians, it changes not! Fulfill God's condition, and He is ever "faithful that promised." Everything depends upon the establishment and acknowledgment of His sovereignty. When the Sun of Righteousness shall arise, there shall surely be healing in His wings. And all this serves to emphasize the great theme of our consideration. As surely as the world can only enjoy peace when it owns His sway, so *the individual sinner must fulfill the same condition* if he would possess peace of heart. Whether God deals with nations or individuals, His activities are based upon eternally inviolate principles. The sinner must lay down his arms of rebellion and proclaim from his heart: "Glory to God in the highest!" Such submission alone can procure the "peace which passeth all understanding."

Peace, perfect peace; in this dark world of sin? The blood of Jesus whispers peace within.

Why do the heathen rage, and the people imagine a vain thing?

The kings of the earth set themselves, and the rulers take counsel together, against the Lord, and against his anointed, saying,

Let us break their bands asunder, and cast away their cords from us.

He that sitteth in the heavens shall laugh: the Lord shall have them in derision.

Then shall he speak unto them in his wrath, and vex them in his sore displeasure.

Yet have I set my king upon my holy hill of Zion.

I will declare the decree: the Lord

hath said unto me, Thou art my Son; this day have I begotten thee.

Ask of me, and I shall give thee the heathen for thine inheritance, and the uttermost parts of the earth for thy possession.

Thou shalt break them with a rod of iron; thou shalt dash them in pieces like a potter's vessel.

Be wise now therefore, O ye kings: be instructed, ye judges of the earth.

Serve the Lord with fear, and rejoice with trembling.

Kiss the Son, lest he be angry, and ye perish from the way, when his wrath is kindled but a little. Blessed are all they that put their trust in him. (Ps. 2:1-11)

CHAPTER XI

HIS SOVEREIGNTY
IN RELATION TO
REPENTANCE

*"Except ye REPENT, ye shall all like-
wise perish."* —Luke 13:3

It may be thought by some that insis-
tence upon the *sovereignty* of Christ as
a condition of salvation rather suggests
that surrender is the instrument of conversion (or life-changing, as emphasized
by a present-day movement). Without
entering into controversy over a much-
disputed subject, it is obvious that there
is a radical difference between surren-
dering in *order to be saved*, and that necessary submission of will which must
ever accompany true *believing*. There is
no need to be confused over terms. The

word "surrender" has come to assume its own technical significance in relation to "victorious life" teaching. The divine message to the sinner is not surrender. It is repent and believe, but this necessarily involves a genuine consent to a new principle of divine government. Surrender without faith leads only to reformation. An initial surrender of will is essential, but subsequent surrender of the whole being to Christ is possible only through the power of a new life already received. This may help to make clear a distinction which, at first, appears almost indiscernible.

Repentance, which is an integral part of the gospel message, is but the negative aspect of the sovereignty of Christ. If salvation is a heart-acknowledgment of His Lordship, it necessarily follows— on the same principle—that sin and self must be dethroned. A true coming to God means that the sinner forsakes *his own way* and turns from *his own* thoughts (Isa. 55:7). This is "repentance toward God," and must ever be linked with "faith toward our Lord Jesus Christ" (Acts 20:21).

The original word for "repent" means to "change one's mind." It involves a new attitude towards sin and toward God. To re-pent is to re-think. It is essential to conversion (Acts 3:19), and is something more than being sorry for sin. Writing to the church at Corinth, Paul rejoices "not that ye were made sorry, but that ye sorrowed *to repentance.*" Apology is not repentance. Scripturally, it implies a definite *change of attitude* to Christ. It is sorrow for sin going so deep that the sinner is willing to turn his back upon his sin and live henceforth "unto righteousness." It is a radical change of mind and heart resulting in transformed conduct. Instead of rejecting Christ it receives Him.

One of the great needs of Christendom today is a genuine return to the preaching of repentance toward God. It is essential to the proclamation of His sovereignty. The Scriptures continually emphasize its importance. The prodigal in Luke 15 passed through deep heart searchings as his conscience was awakened to his sin and folly. "I *have sinned*" was the basis of his plea for mercy.

Repentance was preached by John the Baptist, the disciples, and by the Saviour himself (Matt. 3:2; 4:17; Mark 6:12; Acts 2:38). It was the sum and substance of Paul's testimony to Jew and Gentile alike (Acts 20:21; 26:20). The heart of Christ's parting commission to the twelve was that "repentance and remission of sins be preached to all nations" (Luke 24:47). It is the Lord's supreme desire concerning all men (II Pet. 3:9). Indeed, it is a divine command to all men (Acts 17:30). It is the one and only means of escape from eternal damnation (Luke 13:3-5). Down through the ages the universal appeal of prophets and preachers has been to repentance.

Why is it that this important emphasis is given such a minor place in much of our preaching today? May it not be a subtle stroke of satanic strategy directed against the *sovereignty* of the Saviour? The Holy Spirit links repentance with *faith.* To repent without faith would leave the soul with remorse but no redemption; with sorrow, but no salvation. It would be rather like pumping the ship to get rid of the water without mending the leaks. When the Philippian jailer was converted, he came to the prisoners who had led him to Christ and *washed their stripes.* That was evidence of active repentance.

Repentance must not be translated "penance." It is not meritorious, but exactly the opposite. It is self-judgment, shame, renunciation, and destitution. The interpretation of repentance as "penance" violates its whole meaning. The latter conveys the idea of personal atonement and sacrifice for one's own sin; whereas repentance has to do with the gospel of a finished work, a once-for-all sacrifice for sin. Penance may be nothing but a cloak for sin. Men sin and then *do penance* as a bargain for pardon, only that with an unenlightened conscience they may sin again.

True repentance results in self-abhorrence (Luke 10:13; Joel 2:12-13; Job 42:5-6), while faith in Christ acknowledges His sovereignty. The only evidence of true repentance is "fruit worthy of repentance" (Matt. 3:8; Acts 20:21). This is nothing less than the fruit of the Spirit made possible by the Lordship of Christ

115

in the heart. It is not a repentance to be repented of (II Cor. 7:10). It produces "joy in the presence of the angels" (Luke 15:7, 10). It results in the blotting out of sins (Isa. 55:7; Luke 24:47). It is ever "in the name of the Lord Jesus," and is a condition of receiving the Holy Ghost (Acts 2:38). It is the gift of God (Acts 11:18), so that all human merit is excluded, and is impelled by His goodness (Rom. 2:4).

Thus, the sovereignty of Christ is intimately linked with repentance. Apart from repentance and faith there is no avenue into pardon, life, and fellowship with God.

CHAPTER XII

HIS SOVEREIGNTY
IN RELATION TO
SPIRITUAL INHERITANCE

"Yield yourselves unto God."—Rom. 6:13

When the vital principle of this new sovereignty finds practical expression and the Saviour is "sanctified as Lord" in the hearts of believers, how many problems of life and service find their solution. Those jarring differences which are so often excused on the ground of "natural temperament" soon disappear. Carnal disputes and fleshly judgments, attitudes, actions, and words are given no place. Instead, there is the melting of hearts into a oneness of vision and purpose which results in true spiritual fellowship one with another and with the *Lord*. Thus, the enemy is robbed of his battlefield, and the Lord comes into His own.

May the blessed Holy Spirit bow our hearts low at the Lord's feet in humiliation and self-abasement and then lift writer and reader alike into experimental throne-union with the risen Lord. This is not something extraordinary or extreme, but the normal outworking of this basic and essential condition of the new birth—a recognition of *His sovereignty.* Upon the practical outworking of this principle depends the appropriation of the Christian's spiritual inheritance day by day, and only thus can the Lord himself find His own satisfying portion in His people.

Our one intention through these pages has been to stir up remembrance of the vital meaning of the new birth and the supreme principle of divine sovereignty which is related to it. May the Lord lead us all on into an experimental knowledge of the fact that "blessings abound *where'er He reigns.*" It would be well to trace out the following galaxy of blessings available for every believer, and intimately associated with *His acknowledged kingship* over the believer's entire territory—spirit, soul, and body.

JOY—John 20:20; I Cor. 1:3; II Cor. 10:17; Phil. 3:1, 8; Phil. 4:4, 10

FREEDOM—I Cor. 7:22; Gal. 5:1

FELLOWSHIP—I John 1:7; Phil. 4: 2; I Cor. 10:21

SANCTIFICATION—I Pet. 3:15

VICTORY—Rom. 7:25; I Cor. 15:57; II Pet. 2:9; Jude 9

STABILITY—Phil. 4:1; I Thess. 3:13

EFFECTIVENESS—I Cor. 15:58; Eph. 4:17; II Tim. 2:21

Thus, through yielded and Spirit-filled Christians, the world shall know the impact of such a Gospel as this, both lived and preached; while those whom the Holy Spirit would add to the church shall be led to an initial acknowledgment and ever-growing appreciation of the sovereignty of *"The Christ, the Son of the Living God."*

Great and marvellous are thy works, Lord God Almighty; just and true are thy ways, thou king of saints. Who shall fear thee, O Lord, and glorify thy name? for thou only art holy. (Rev. 15:3-4)

Crown Him with many crowns,
　　The Lamb upon the Throne,
Hark, how the Heavenly anthem drowns,
　　All music but its own;
Awake, my soul, and sing,
　　Of Him, Who died for thee,
And hail HIM as thy Matchless KING,
　　Throughout Eternity.

　　　　　　　　　　　Amen and Amen